1

Cover Design by Chris Jamerson, NHANCE GRAPHICS
Interior Design by Sandra Ballenger, Design by Sandra

Kingdom Leadership Development Publishing
Munster, IN
www.kingdomld.org

TABLE OF CONTENTS

ANSWERING THE CALL

Men and women seeking to serve, lead and love with excellence at every level and in all aspects of life have the ability to make their jobs look relatively easy, particularly from the perspectives of those who choose to observe from afar. We, who resign ourselves to view objectively these extraordinary leaders through the lens of a more watchful eye, must realize that to lead others with purpose, one must have the intestinal fortitude of a powerful lion, the resiliency of a focused ant, and the temperament of a gentle lamb in order to endure and embrace the successes and failures that accompany the role of true leadership.

MINISTRY IS NOT ALWAYS FUN

There is a big difference between the things you "get" to do and the things you "have" to do.

Ecclesiastes 5:3 (AMP)

"For a dream comes with much business and painful effort, and a fool's voice with many words."

Recall a time when serving at church was "not fun." How did you handle it? Briefly describe the effect that period of time had on your personal call to serve in ministry.

_____

_____

_____

_____

Spend a few minutes meditating on Ecclesiastes 5:3, then answer the following questions:

o   Can hard work or painful effort be avoided?_____

o   What system(s) do you have in place to maintain your "yes" to God when serving Him isn't fun?

_____

_____

_____

_____

BE A FOLLOWER NOT A FAN

Real leaders desire followers—not fans. Fans "worship" you, but followers "work with" you.

Philippians 4:9 (KJV)

"Those things, which ye have both learned, and received, and heard, and seen in me, do: and the God of peace shall be with you."

Identify three of your Pastor's core values when it comes to serving, leading and loving.

_____

_____

_____

How do you personally exemplify those values and pass them on to others?

_____

_____

_____

Review Philippians 4:9. Describe certain principles from your Pastor/Leader that you have:

Learned in a sermon and imparted to others.

_____

Heard in passing and spoken to others.

_____

Seen and demonstrated to others.

_____

DO NOT JUDGE ANOTHER MAN'S SERVANT

The Bible is very clear about our opinions as they pertain to someone else's servant.

Romans 14:4 (AMP)

"Who are you to pass judgment on and censure another's household servant? It is before his own master that he stands or falls. And he shall stand and be upheld, for the Master (the Lord) is mighty to support him and make him stand."

Mark 9:38 (MSG)

"John spoke up, 'Teacher, we saw a man using your name to expel demons and we stopped him because he wasn't in our group.'"

Not everyone measures up to our own personal standards and most of us, being products of our environments, have a tendency to develop a sense of what we believe is a "proper" way to do things. With this in mind, what do you think was in the Apostle John's heart when he made the statement in Mark 3:8?

_____

_____

_____

_____

What do you think is the difference between a gap in competence and purposeful wickedness?

_____

_____

_____

_____

Examine these scriptural methods below then contemplate how they might look in your ministry life.

2 Timothy 2:2 (AMP)

"And the [instructions] which you have heard from me along with many witnesses, transmit and entrust [as a deposit] to reliable and faithful men who will be competent and qualified to teach others also."

Romans 12:16-18 (AMP)

"Live in harmony with one another; do not be haughty (snobbish, high-minded, exclusive), but readily adjust yourself to [people, things] and give yourselves to humble tasks. Never overestimate yourself or be wise in your own conceits. Repay no one evil for evil, but take thought for what is honest and proper and noble [aiming to be above reproach] in the sight of everyone. If possible, as far as it depends on you, live at peace with everyone."

MOSES' CALL/THE UNDER-QUALIFIED

Like Moses, most of us have every excuse as to why God should choose someone else.

1 Corinthians 1:26-31 (KJV)

"For ye see your calling, brethren, how that not many wise men after the flesh, not many mighty, not many noble, are called. But God hath chosen the foolish things of the world to confound the wise; and God hath chosen the weak things of the world to confound the things which are mighty; And base things of the world, and things which are despised, hath God chosen, yea, and things which are not, to bring to nought things that are: That no flesh should glory in his presence. But of him are ye in Christ Jesus, who of God is made unto us wisdom, and righteousness, and sanctification, and redemption: That, according as it is written, He that glorieth, let him glory in the Lord."

Have you, like Moses, ever doubted your ability to lead others? List some of the reasons you may have felt unqualified for leadership.

_____

_____

_____

_____

Read 1 Corinthians 1:26-31 again and review your list. Allow God to show you how He could get the glory from those same reasons.

Now, mentally evaluate yourself and past practices. Do you, as a leader, look for people with obvious abilities to serve with you? In what ways could our desire to win or to look good overshadow and/or hinder our desire to bring God glory? Are you willing to select those who are unlearned, weak and unknown to serve with you? Think on these things.

PETER'S CALL/THE QUALIFIED

God will use the very tools, talents, gifting, and anointing we use to make a living, and call upon those things for His purpose.

Matthew 4:19 (AMP)

"And He said to them, 'Come after Me [as disciples—letting Me be your Guide], follow Me, and I will make you fishers of men!'"

In Luke 5, Peter was asked to lend Jesus his boat. Have you ever lent Jesus your "boat" by giving your marketable talents or skills to the church or ministry? If so, what did it cost you and what did you gain?

_____

_____

_____

_____

List some of the vocational skills you can offer to the Kingdom

○ _____

○ _____

○ _____

○ _____

PAUL'S CALL/THE OVER-QUALIFIED

When God calls you, bring all that you have learned up until that time. Bring all of your skills, education, and experiences and then lay them at the feet of Jesus as an offering.

Philippians 3:8 (AMP)

"Yes, furthermore, I count everything as loss compared to the possession of the priceless privilege (the overwhelming preciousness, the surpassing worth, and supreme advantage) of knowing Christ Jesus my Lord and of progressively becoming more deeply and intimately acquainted with Him [of perceiving and recognizing and

understanding Him more fully and clearly]. For His sake I have lost everything and consider it all to be mere rub-bish (refuse, dregs), in order that I may win (gain) Christ (the Anointed One)."

Though our admirable qualifications are notable achievements, when God calls us it is vital that we learn to lay those things aside and put them "on a shelf" so to speak. By doing this, we may allow the Holy Spirit to educate us concerning His Kingdom.

How do you suppose our qualifications can get in the way of walking by faith:

When asked to submit to someone with less education or experience than you?

_____

_____

_____

When God gives you unconditional solutions?

_____

_____

When an opportunity to serve someone who doesn't seem to deserve your time?

_____

_____

Why do you think the Amplified Bible defines the word "fool" as self-confident?

_____

_____

BE BOLD

Don't get stuck waiting for a burning bush experience. Follow that still, small voice and step forth in obedience where you believe God is leading you.

Romans 7:21 (KJV)

"I find then a law, that, when I would do good, evil is present with me."

Matthew 14:22-24 (AMP)

"Then He directed the disciples to get into the boat and go before Him to the other side, while He sent away the crowds. And after He had dismissed the multitudes, He went up into the hills by Himself to pray. When it was

evening, He was still there alone. But the boat was by this time out on the sea, many furlongs [a furlong is one-eighth of a mile] distant from the land, beaten and tossed by the waves, for the wind was against them."

John 16:33 (AMP)

"I have told you these things, so that in Me you may have [perfect] peace and confidence. In the world you have tribulation and trials and distress and frustration; but be of good cheer [take courage; be confident, certain, undaunted]! For I have overcome the world. [I have deprived it of power to harm you and have conquered it for you.]"

Recall situations (no names please) where outside forces that were sent to cause you to doubt your assignment and your God, manifested the themselves.

People:

○ _____

○ _____

○ _____

Natural circumstances:

○ _____

○ _____

Spiritual opposition:

○ _____

○ _____

As we consider such things, we must expect the challenges of this world and prepare to meet them; however, realize that preparation may only come through hearing, reading, studying, meditating and praying God's Word. As spiritually prepared believers in His truths and promises, we can become like Paul, taking pleasure in our infirmities and accepting our weaknesses.

2 Corinthians 12:10 (KJV)

"Therefore, I take pleasure in infirmities, in reproaches, in necessities, in persecutions, in distresses for Christ's sake: for when I am weak, then am I strong."

2 Corinthians 12:10 (GW)

"Therefore, I accept weakness, mistreatment, hardship, persecution, and difficulties suffered for Christ. It's clear that when I'm weak, I'm strong."

Remember: If our testing was easy, if there were no challenges, if it didn't require faith, then it wasn't God's call!

Luke 9:62 (AMP)
"Jesus said to him, No one who puts his hand to the plow and looks back [to the things behind] is fit for the kingdom of God."

✓ I will carry my leader's heart and transmit it others.

✓ Wickedness and incompetence are two different things and I handle both according to the Word of God.

✓ God chose me because I am the perfect candidate to give him Glory!

✓ I willingly lend my talents and skills to Kingdom work.

✓ I am willing to put all I think I know on a shelf in order to learn from Jesus.

✓ Jesus has already overcome every challenge I will face while on my assignment from Him.

✓ I boldly and confidently give God an irreversible YES!

PREPARE TO WEAR THE EPHOD

The Ephod is a sacred vestment worn by high priests. For our purposes, it represents the priesthood portion of your work in ministry. When we speak about preparing to wear the ephod, we are talking about preparing ourselves to represent God and serve people. Though our salvation is secure, it is critical to our ministries that we continue to prepare daily, allowing our hearts to be washed with God's Word so that we may wear this spiritual garment worthily.

TAKE A BATH

If you skip enough baths, after a while the people around you will be able to tell—your attitude will stink.

2Timothy 2:21 (AMP)

"So whoever cleanses himself [from what is ignoble and unclean, who separates himself from contact with contaminating and corrupting influences] will [then himself] be a vessel set apart and useful for honorable and noble purposes, consecrated and profitable to the Master, fit and ready for any good work."

Identify your set time and place that you spend with God in His Word in order to receive cleansing. If you don't already have one, imagine it and write it down.

_____

_____

As you are "cleansed" and "repeatedly pruned" during your alone time with God and His Word, what struggles have been or are being purged from your life as a result (see John 15:1-5, the Amplified Bible)?

_____

_____

_____

THE WORD IS A MIRROR

The Word of God will show you yourself (and where you are lacking) in no uncertain terms; however, it will also give you wisdom and power to make any needed adjustments so you can face the day with confidence.

2 Corinthians 3:18 (AMP)

"And all of us, as with unveiled face, [because we] continued to behold [in the Word of God] as into a mirror the glory of the Lord, are constantly being transfigured into His very own image in ever increasing splendor and from one degree of glory to another; [for this comes] from the Lord [Who is] the Spirit."

What do you think is the difference between "glancing at" a mirror and "staring into" the mirror"?

_____

_____

_____

The definition of the word meditate is to contemplate or plan, consider, design or dream; a related word is "chew." Reading James 1:23-25, can a person carefully and thoughtfully meditate on the Word, looking into it as if it were a mirror and then simply forget it? Explain:

_____

_____

_____

_____

How are we different when remembering God's Word vs. forgetting what we read?

_____

_____

_____

Philippians 1:6 (AMP)

"And I am convinced and sure of this very thing, that He Who began a good work in you will continue until the day of Jesus Christ [right up to the time of His return], developing [that good work] and perfecting and bringing it to full completion in you."

THE WORD BRINGS FAITH

The church is the greatest threat to Satan's kingdom, and he will fight you every step of the way to keep you from being successful.

Joshua 1:8 (AMP)

"This Book of the Law shall not depart out of your mouth, but you shall meditate on it day and night, that you may observe and do according to all that is written in it. For then you shall make your way prosperous, and then you shall deal wisely and have good success."

What projects or goals are you working on that seem insurmountable right now?

_____

_____

_____

What promise(s) from the Word of God can you apply to your guaranteed success?

_____

_____

_____

Whom will you ask to agree with you?

_____

_____

BE AVAILABLE

Always be available for God to use you in ways outside of your "job," and be willing to put down the "task at hand" for a moment.

2 Chronicles 16:9 (MSG)

"God is always on the alert, constantly on the lookout for people who are totally committed to Him. You were foolish to go for human help when you could have had God's help. Now you're in trouble—one round of war after another."

What does this scripture verse say about God's willingness to come to the rescue of people who love Him?

_____

_____

_____

Why do you think people seek help from others before going to God first?

_____

_____

_____

Who does God use to answer prayers?

_____

_____

2Timothy 2:4 (AMP)

"No soldier when in service gets entangled in the enterprises of [civilian] life; his aim is to satisfy and please the one who enlisted him."

Considering 2Timothy 2:4, what things could cause you to be unavailable to God's request?

_____

_____

_____

_____

"Don't be so busy with ministry that you miss an opportunity to minister!" -Dr. Pam Ross

COMMIT TO PERSONAL EXCELLENCE

Excellence in Holiness

What do the following two passages teach us about the necessity, benefits and pathway to holiness?

Psalm 24:3-5 (AMP)

"Who shall go up into the mountain of the Lord? Or who shall stand in His Holy Place? He who has clean hands and a pure heart, who has not lifted himself up to falsehood or to what is false, nor sworn deceitfully. He shall receive blessing from the Lord and righteousness from the God of his salvation."

Galatians 3:11 (KJV)

"But that no man is justified by the law in the sight of God, it is evident: for, The just shall live by faith."

_____

_____

_____

_____

Excellence in Stewardship

Using the scale below rate how satisfied are you with your personal stewardship. Enter 1, 2, 3 or 4 next to each statement.

1 - Strongly Disagree   2 - Disagree   3 - Agree   4 - Strongly Agree

_____ I am living well within my current manifested means; tithing, saving and giving as God directs, increasing more and more.

_____ I accomplish what God puts before me each day. I am moving steadily toward my long-term goals. I have no problems saying "yes" to the right things and "no" to the wrong things.

_____ I take responsibility for increasing my gifts and talents through reading, relationships and revelation.

_____ I'm not comfortable developing relationships.

_____ I'm still learning to trust God when it comes to tithes and offerings.

_____ I don't know what my gifts are.

_____ It has never occurred to me to set goals for my life.

Excellence in Discipline - Adhering to a Pre-Set Decision or Pre-Defined Order

Daniel 6:10 (AMP)

"Now when Daniel knew that the writing was signed, he went into his house, and his windows being open in his chamber toward Jerusalem, he got down upon his knees three times a day and prayed and gave thanks before his God, as he had done previously."

What are your best habits?

_____

_____

_____

_____

How long did it take you to develop those habits?

_____

_____

Are there any other good habits you'd like to form? Please elaborate.

_____

_____

_____

Isaiah 6:5-8 (AMP)

"Then said I, Woe is me! For I am undone and ruined, because I am a man of unclean lips, and I dwell in the midst of a people of unclean lips; for my eyes have seen the King, the Lord of hosts! Then flew one of the seraphim [heavenly beings] to me, having a live coal in his hand which he had taken with tongs from off the altar; And with it he touched my mouth and said, Behold, this has touched your lips; your iniquity and guilt are taken away, and your sin is completely atoned for and forgiven. Also I heard the voice of the Lord, saying, Whom shall I send? And who will go for Us? Then said I, Here am I; send me."

God will do what is necessary to prepare you, because He needs YOU.

NOW YOU KNOW

✓   **I will spend time in the Word of God daily.**

✓   **Meditation is key to effective time with God...Chew and Do!**

✓   **The issues in my own life will not stop me from being available to God.**

✓   **I receive God's grace for clean hands and a pure heart.**

✓   **God is teaching me how to handle my money, time, gifts and talents in a better manner.**

✓   **I make high-pressure decisions in low pressure atmospheres.**

✓   **God wants and needs me for His Kingdom plan!**

CHRISTIANITY IS A TEAM SPORT

We were introduced to the concept of teamwork when God first said, "Let us…" (Genesis 1:26). Here we learn about the three-in-One nature of our Holy God—Father, Son, and Spirit—eternally working together and demonstrating divine submission to fulfill the ultimate sovereign plan. With each of us having been made in God's image, we must strive to work in the same manner, having our own souls and bodies learning to submit to our newly-created spirits upon salvation. It is at this point that we learn to work with others as a succinct body of believers (the church), harmoniously loving and helping others by the leading of the Holy Spirit with Christ the Lord at the helm, submitting to our faithful God and Father. It is indeed a team sport.

SONS AND BROTHERS

Two are always better than one. When you are working alone, there can appear to be no end to your labor.

Ecclesiastes 4:8 (AMP)

"Here is one alone—no one with him; he neither has child nor brother..."

NO CHILD – Sadly, this person in Ecclesiastes 4:8 hasn't identified, developed or deployed anyone.

NO BROTHER – Neither has this person connected or developed a network of colleagues.

Our omniscient God knows the importance of working alongside someone; consequently, we discover that traveling in twos is a pattern we see in Kingdom business. Read the following Scripture verses and explain why you think it is important to work as a team.

Mark 6:7 - Jesus sent them out two by two

Luke 10:1 -Jesus sent the 70 out two by two

Matthew 18:19 - If any two agree ...

_____

_____

_____

Meditate on Ecclesiastes 4:8, then list those whom you consider sons and brothers in your circle (they may or may not be related to you):

_____

_____

THE CONSEQUECES OF GOING IT ALONE

A victory, when accomplished alone, can feel like just another thing to check off your "to-do" list.

Ecclesiastes 4:8 (AMP)

"Here is one alone—no one with him; he neither has child nor brother. Yet there is no end to all his labor, neither is his eye satisfied with riches, neither does he ask, For whom do I labor and deprive myself of good? This is also vanity (emptiness, falsity, and futility); yes, it is a painful effort and an unhappy business."

These are some of the symptoms leaders experience when who choosing to go it alone:

o   often overwhelmed

o   little or no satisfaction with success

o   lose sight of purpose

o   spirit of heaviness

How may partnering with others help leaders in these areas?

_____

_____

Have you ever had a bad experience that discouraged you from wanting to connect with others? Briefly describe that episode:

_____

_____

_____

_____

THE MANDATE TO MENTOR

Just as we expect God to supply all of our needs according to His riches in glory by Christ Jesus (Philippians 4:19), we should also expect Him to send us excellent people to help us, people who have the skills, talents, anointing and resources that we ourselves may not have.

Meditate: The first thing Jesus did after His ordination, baptism, and temptation was build a team! How did He do it? Why did He do it? What were His anticipated results?

Mark 3:13-15 (AMP)

"And He went up on the hillside and called to Him [for Himself] those whom He wanted and chose, and they came to Him. And He appointed twelve to continue to be with Him, and that He might send them out to preach [as apostles or special messengers] and to have authority and power to heal the sick and to drive out demons."

o   How: He called those He wanted

o   Why: to be with Him (assist Him)

o   What: to have authority and power…

What personality, gifting, anointing, skills, and interests are MOST WANTED for your team? MAKE ROOM!

This is an example of a "Most Wanted" poster done by our Bible College students for a compassion project.

Note: this group was looking for someone that loves Jesus AND people, with a big heart, easy-going (flexible), a beautiful and warm smile, and a listening ear.

LEARN TO SPOT POTENTIAL

A true leader is able to recognize the potential in others.

Matthew 4:19 (AMP)

"And He said to them, Come after Me [as disciples—letting Me be your Guide], follow Me, and I will make you fishers of men!"

Just as Jesus knew the potential of those He chose—what they would be doing paled by comparison to what they would eventually become—so it is with leaders that select people to work with them, as well. Always remember that people often show up as raw material. It is what they will grow to become in God's kingdom that is most important!

In light of Matthew 4:19, list some areas where you have personally grown while serving in ministry.

_____

_____

_____

_____

Apostolic leadership raises others up and sends them out to fulfill their God-givens dreams.

Luke 22:31-32 (AMP)

"Simon, Simon (Peter), listen! Satan has asked excessively that [all of] you be given up to him [out of the power and keeping of God], that he might sift [all of] you like grain, But I have prayed especially for you [Peter], that your [own] faith may not fail; and when you yourself have turned again, strengthen and establish your brethren."

Dedicate one hour a week to developing someone else - Luke 6:38

Expect a 360 degree return - Galatians 6:7

Develop the apostolic gene - Romans 1:11-12

Romans 1:11-12 (AMP)

"For I am yearning to see you, that I may impart and share with you some spiritual gift to strengthen and establish you; That is, that we may be mutually strengthened and encouraged and comforted by each other's faith, both yours and mine."

A NECESSITY TO NETWORK

"I'm a movement by myself, ooh

But I'm a force when we're together

Mami, I'm good all by myself, ooh

But baby, you, you make me better"

-You Make Me Better by Fabolous

If the world is sensible enough to know that having someone else can make them better, as is mentioned in the lyrics by John David Jackson (aka Fabolous), then how much more impact should God's Word have on those who believe?

Make time to connect with other people who are serving in the Kingdom; for God has called others to make you better.

Take an inventory of your network. Meditate on the Scripture verses below, then answer the questions that immediately follow:

Genesis 2:18 (AMP)

"Now the Lord God said, It is not good (sufficient, satisfactory) that the man should be alone; I will make him a helper meet (suitable, adapted, complementary) for him."

Who can help me?

_____

_____

Proverbs 27:5-6 (AMP)

"Open rebuke is better than love that is hidden. Faithful are the wounds of a friend, but the kisses of an enemy are lavish and deceitful."

Who can rebuke me?

_____

_____

Proverbs 27:9-10 (AMP)

"Oil and perfume rejoice the heart; so does the sweetness of a friend's counsel that comes from the heart. Your own friend and your father's friend, forsake them not; neither go to your brother's house in the day of your calamity. Better is a neighbor who is near [in spirit] than a brother who is far off [in heart]."

Who can advise me on matters of the heart?

_____

_____

Proverbs 27:17 (AMP)

"Iron sharpens iron; so a man sharpens the countenance of his friend [to show rage or worthy purpose]."

Who can challenge me?

_____

_____

Ecclesiastes 4:9-10 (MSG)

"It's better to have a partner than go it alone. Share the work, share the wealth; and if one falls down, the other helps, but if there's no one to help, tough!"

NOW YOU KNOW

✓   **Every assignment requires a team. Build it!**

✓   **Use discernment to connect to the right people.**

✓   **The being of ministry outweighs the knowing and doing of it.**

✓   **I am opened to being Helped! Rebuked! Advised! Challenged!**

✓   **Success isn't success without a successor.**

THE LITTLE RED HEN SYNDROME

There are many well-meaning, Holy Ghost-filled, Bible-believing people that live by the spiritual ideology which dictates that our wellbeing and suffering is based on what WE do. This is not necessarily a bad principle when used in the correct Biblical context; for there is indeed a consequence to every decision we make. However, we must be careful not to neglect the sheer goodness of the Lord that is based not on OUR doing, but on HIS. Without HIM, we can do nothing (John 15:5).

THE LITTLE RED HEN

If you don't work, you don't get the blessing!

Is the above statement true or false? _____

Is it a reflection of Kingdom culture? _____

Many church folks are just like the Little Red Hen who worked relentlessly to bake her bread. To her dismay no one helped and, therefore, no one earned the right to share her bread. Let's examine the following passages from Matthew, John, and Luke where people received provision, mercy and favor that they did NOT work for. What can we learn from each incident?

Matthew 14:16 (AMP)

"Jesus said, 'They do not need to go away; you give them something to eat.'"

_____

_____

_____

John 8:11 (AMP)

"She answered, No one, Lord! And Jesus said, 'I do not condemn you either. Go on your way and from now on sin no more.'"

_____

_____

_____

Luke 19:5 (AMP)

"And when Jesus reached the place, He looked up and said to him, 'Zacchaeus, hurry and come down; for I must stay at your house today.'"

_____

_____

_____

Isaiah 55:1 (AMP)

"WAIT and listen, everyone who is thirsty! Come to the waters; and he who has no money, come, buy and eat! Yes, come, buy [priceless, spiritual] wine and milk without money and without price [simply for the self-surrender that accepts the blessing]."

THE SIN OF THE OLDER BROTHER

A "religious" way of thinking (legalistic) generally produces a "works" mentality. This can make it difficult for us to believe that God wants us to have any fun at all.

Read the account in Luke 15:11-32. What was the sin of the older brother?

_____

_____

_____

What was the older brother's perspective of the father's party?

_____

_____

_____

What was the Father's perspective?

_____

_____

_____

Meditate - What do you think God requires when we have blown it?

_____

_____

_____

Micah 6:6-8 (KJV)

"Wherewith shall I come before the LORD, and bow myself before the high God? Shall I come before him with burnt offerings, with calves of a year old? Will the LORD be pleased with thousands of rams, or with ten thousands of rivers of oil? Shall I give my firstborn for my transgression, the fruit of my body for the sin of my soul? He hath shewed thee, O man, what is good; and what doth the LORD require of thee, but to do justly, and to love mercy, and to walk humbly with thy God?"

o   Do what is right. Give to God and others the good that is due them.

o   Love the mercy shown to others. "Justice is the friend of the innocent. Mercy is the friend of the guilty."-Bishop TD Jakes

o   Humbly receive the sacrifice of Jesus who died for your sins, then allow the Spirit of the Lord to show you how to live God's way.

Jonah 4:10-11 (AMP)

"Then said the Lord, 'You have had pity on the gourd, for which you have not labored nor made it grow, which came up in a night and perished in a night. And should not I spare Nineveh, that great city, in which there are

more than 120,000 persons not [yet old enough to] know their right hand from their left, and also many cattle [not accountable for sin]?'"

Why do you think it is sometimes difficult to love mercy when God displays it to others?

_____

_____

_____

As servant leaders, we must meet our responsibilities without being in bondage to them.

MARTHA, MARTHA!

What is it about us "responsible" folks that can make us value our working FOR the Lord more than a relationship WITH the Lord? God's desire is that we not simply be servants, but also that we be sons and daughters in relationship with Him.

Are you more comfortable working than resting?

Do you feel more "holy" mourning and fasting than celebrating and feasting?

Are you irritated with lazy people?

Meditate - the Bible says Martha was distracted with much serving. How do you know when your responsibilities in the church are distracting you from what Jesus is saying?

_____

_____

_____

Luke 19:44 (AMP)

"And they will dash you down to the ground, you [Jerusalem] and your children within you; and they will not leave in you one stone upon another, [all] because you did not come progressively to recognize and know and understand [from observation and experience] the time of your visitation [that is, when God was visiting you, the time in which God showed Himself gracious toward you and offered you salvation through Christ]."

The above scripture is in reference to salvation and teaches a lesson of unnecessary suffering that comes when we miss what God is freely offering us.

RECEIVE THE FAVOR

That Little Red Hen who valued hard work wasn't necessarily wrong for not sharing her bread with those she felt didn't deserve any, but she (like many believers) lacked the understanding of true grace and mercy that—despite our mishaps—God faithfully and consistently pours upon each of us because of HIS righteousness. As servant leaders who ALWAYS represent Christ Jesus and seek to be like Him, we will be confronted by the prodigals and the resentful hard workers at every turn. When we observe what might be perceived as an unde-served blessing, know that God's grace is in full effect.

Psalms 35:27 (AMP)

"Let those who favor my righteous cause and have pleasure in my uprightness shout for joy and be glad and say continually, 'Let the Lord be magnified, Who takes pleasure in the prosperity of His servant.'"

Romans 8:31-32 (AMP)

"What then shall we say to [all] this? If God is for us, who [can be] against us? [Who can be our foe, if God is on our side?] He who did not withhold or spare [even] His own Son but gave Him up for us all, will He not also with Him freely and graciously give us all [other] things?"

Luke 12:32 (KJV)

"Fear not, little flock; for it is your Father's good pleasure to give you the kingdom."

According to the above Scripture verses, describe how God?

_____

_____

NOW YOU KNOW

✓   **The blessing of God is a reflection of His nature, not ours. (Matt 5:45)**

✓   **God's resources are unlimited.**

✓   **We can keep a grace mentality while doing the works of God.**

✓   **Leaders are called to pave the way for others to believe and receive.**

✓   **It's important to get happy about what God is happy about.**

MATURE THROUGH THE MANURE

Unless you are someone who can appreciate the wonders of agriculture, "manure" will not be an attractive word, to say the least. In fact, you might think it's downright offensive. Those who value it as an organic matter simply used as fertilizer, learn early on that manure is extremely beneficial to the whole of society. In the same way, when confronted with certain issues that appear unattractive, highly offensive, and seemingly useless, maturity is reached and we are spiritually strengthened to handle tough situations, when we learn to view them through the eyes of Jesus.

THE CHOICE IS YOURS

Everything you accomplish for God will require you to be strong. Needing to always verbally express a compliant is a weakness.

If you've ever encountered manure, you know that you have at least three choices.

1. Be the victim and take it with you everywhere you go.

2. Dedicate your life to tracking down the dog that did it.

3. Wipe it off and move on.

As you read the following Scripture verses, think about how you have handled offenses in the past. Then, consider the role the Word of God plays in the lives of those who trust in Him.

Ephesians 4:26 (AMP)

"When angry, do not sin; do not ever let your wrath (your exasperation, your fury or indignation) last until the sun goes down."

Hebrews 1:3 (AMP)

"...upholding and maintaining and guiding and propelling the universe by His mighty word of power."

Being made in His image, our personal worlds are "upheld, maintained, guided, and propelled" by the words that we use. Identify three situations that might prompt a negative response—words, actions or thoughts, i.e., "slow or stopped traffic puts me in a bad mood all day" or "he never admits to being wrong, but this time I'm going to let him have it!"

1) _____

_____

2) _____

_____

3) _____

_____

In his best-selling book, *The 7 Habits of Highly Effective People*, author Steven Covey teaches about the gap between stimulus and response. Mr. Covey examines our unique ability as humans to pause and choose what we will think, say and do. Unfortunately, many times we neglect to do just that—pause and give ourselves time to think first, and then choose how we will respond when confronted with scenarios that make us extremely uncomfortable.

James 1:19 (AMP)

"Understand [this], my beloved brethren. Let every man be quick to hear [a ready listener], slow to speak, slow to take offense and to get angry."

Leaders should learn to assess the situation from a Godly perspective so that we may respond in ways that build us up spiritually. We can't always choose the situations we find ourselves in, but we can ALWAYS pause and choose how we respond.

Revisit the three situations you previously identified. The next time you are confronted, will you be able to confine the anger you feel, and refrain from sinning verbally or in your thoughts? Can you now think first and pre-determine what words will come out of your mouth? This takes consistent practice and, most likely, we will have many opportunities to get good at it. Keep in mind that responding graciously is definitely achievable for the servant leader whose goal is to lead like Christ.

Pray and ask God to provide you with a strategic plan that will help you to face your enemy (who is ultimately the devil according Ephesians 6:4) and conquer the situation. Say to yourself, "The next time this happens I will _____."

GET TO KNOW GOD

Getting to know God requires walking with Him through often unpleasant circumstances.

Daniel 11:32 (KJV)

"... but the people that do know their God shall be strong, and do exploits."

Many times the difficulties we encounter—sickness, financial lack, emotional pain, etc.—cause us to reach out to God. The good news is these fearful situations can catapult us into prayer and, thereby, help us to know Him intimately and in greater ways.

Meditate: In what way(s) will YOU need to know God in order to complete YOUR ministry assignment?

_____

_____

_____

_____

_____

Proverbs 17:17 (KJV)

"A friend loveth at all times, and a brother is born for adversity."

Pay strict attention to the phrase AT ALL TIMES. Jesus set the example: He never stops loving us despite our inadequacies. His relationship to those who receive His love is the epitome of friendship. In the form of man, He was the first to be resurrected to eternal life, making Him the "first of many brethren" (Romans 8:29) who promises never to leave us (Psalm 9:9; Hebrews 13:5). Make a commitment to LOVE GOD BACK to the best of your ability in whatever season you encounter, and trust Him just as much in times of adversity as you do in the wonderful seasons of life.

Genesis 18:17 (AMP)

"And the Lord said, 'Shall I hide from Abraham [My friend and servant] what I am going to do?'"

Based on Proverbs 17:17 why do you think God called Abraham his friend?

_____

_____

_____

_____

Jesus, our Lord, refers to His disciples as His friends.

John 15:15 (AMP)

"I do not call you servants (slaves) any longer; for the servant does not know what his master is doing (working out). But I have called you My friends, because I have made known to you everything that I have heard from My Father. [I have revealed to you everything that I have learned from Him.]"

Knowing the promises of the Lord, revisit Proverbs 17:17 to complete the following statements:

"He loves me _____."

"He is with me _____."

MATURE THROUGH THE MANURE

God expects us to be fruitful in every season, so we can expect to be strengthened right smack in the middle of the manure!

Luke 13:6-9 (AMP)

"And He told them this parable: A certain man had a fig tree, planted in his vineyard, and he came looking for fruit on it, but did not find [any]. So he said to the vinedresser, See here! For these three years I have come looking for fruit on this fig tree and I find none. Cut it down! Why should it continue also to use up the ground [to deplete the soil, intercept the sun, and take up room]? But he replied to him, Leave it alone, sir, [just] this one more year, till I dig around it and put manure [on the soil]. Then perhaps it will bear fruit after this; but if not, you can cut it down and out."

John 16:33 (AMP)

"I have told you these things, so that in Me you may have [perfect] peace and confidence. In the world you have tribulation and trials and distress and frustration; but be of good cheer [take courage; be confident, certain, undaunted]! For I have overcome the world. [I have deprived it of power to harm you and have conquered it for you.]"

Let's revisit some of the trials, distress and frustration in your life in light of the Scriptures.

What fruit (Godly attributes) does God expect you to produce when facing these challenges (see Galatians 5:22-23)?

_____

_____

_____

_____

God empowers us to be fruitful.

Zechariah 4:6 (AMP)

"Then he said to me, 'This [addition of the bowl to the candlestick, causing it to yield a ceaseless supply of oil from the olive trees] is the word of the Lord to Zerubbabel, saying, Not by might, nor by power, but by My Spirit [of Whom the oil is a symbol],' says the Lord of hosts."

John 15:5 (AMP)

"I am the Vine; you are the branches. Whoever lives in Me and I in him bears much (abundant) fruit. However, apart from Me [cut off from vital union with Me] you can do nothing."

- ✓ The enemy brings negative forces in our lives in hopes of producing negative words, thoughts, and actions.

- ✓ God allows us to face negative forces to strengthen and mature us.

- ✓ We can decide how we will respond to negative situations.

- ✓ We get to know God best in difficult seasons.

- ✓ We are committed to loving God at all times.

- ✓ Our fruitfulness is determined by our ability to stay connected to the anointing.

CHRISTIAN CUSSING

If you consistently serve in any capacity of church ministry, then you are well aware that there are times when that "old man" wants to be resurrected and let out a few choice words that the devil taught us to use when faced with adversity. As new creatures in Christ, no longer under the influence of Satan's destructive way of resolving issues, we struggle with another set of words that challenge our way of thinking and are vital to helping us accomplish our mission.

THE "B" WORD - BALANCE

Mention the word "balance" to a dedicated servant-leader and he or she will look at you like you just spit out a frog!

1 Peter 5:8 (AMP)

"Be well balanced (temperate, sober of mind), be vigilant and cautious at all times; for that enemy of yours, the devil, roams around like a lion roaring [in fierce anger], seeking someone to seize upon and devour."

Always keep in mind that the enemy can devour anyone who is out of balance; therefore, it is imperative that we periodically weigh our souls (mind, will, emotions) to ensure that we are maintaining a healthy balance in every aspect of our lives.

JUMP ON THE SCALE AND START WEIGHING!

My regular time alone with God is:

_____

The last time I had dinner and a movie (or something enjoyable) with my spouse was:

_____

The last time I did something fun with my children was:

_____

The last time I scheduled a medical or dental appointment was:

_____

On a scale of 1 to 10 my satisfaction with the cleanliness of my home and lawn is at:

_____

I am on time for my appointments whether on the job or personal:

_____Always _____Frequently _____Sometimes _____Rarely

I pay my bills on time:

_____Always _____Frequently _____Sometimes _____Rarely

If our stance in life is off balance, then every area of our existence will be affected. If we lean too much on our work, then our health may suffer. If we spend all of our time praying, when would our work ever get done? Don't be offended by the word "balance" but instead, embrace it; otherwise, you will be one stressed-out believer! Why? Because your underlying values (things that are extremely important to you) are not being met.

When your actions don't line up with your values, the result is stress. In the spaces below, write down your top five (5) values:

1. _____

2. _____

3. _____

4. _____

5. _____

Now, take a look at your calendar and checkbook. Does either of them reflect your core values?

Recognize that there should always be a healthy tension between what you **want** to do vs. what you **need** to do. For example, if you attempt to relieve the tension between family and work by spending all of your time with family, you will inevitably risk losing your job. In the same way, if you spend all of your time on the job—whether secular or in the church—then your personal life will suffer greatly.

Let's review the three-step process!

1 Peter 5:6-8 (AMP)

"Therefore humble yourselves [demote, lower yourselves in your own estimation] under the mighty hand of God, that in due time He may exalt you; casting the whole of your care [all your anxieties, all your worries, all your concerns, once and for all] on Him, for He cares for you affectionately and cares about you watchfully. Be well balanced (temperate, sober of mind), be vigilant and cautious at all times; for that enemy of yours, the devil, roams around like a lion roaring [in fierce hunger], seeking someone to seize upon and devour."

1. How can humility keep us balanced?

_____

_____

_____

2. According to the above Scripture verses, what is our motivation for casting our care on God?

_____

_____

3. In what way can the enemy take advantage of an unbalanced, unwatchful believer?

_____

_____

THE "S" WORD - SLEEP

Working hard is admirable, but being a workaholic is more detrimental to our work ethic than one might think. Many of us pride ourselves in working to the extreme and getting the job done at all costs, even if we have to lose sleep doing it. When the family is settled in and the house is calm and quiet, it's an ideal time to get some quality work done; but that should be reserved only for a once-in-a-while project—not every night! We often lose sight of the harm we often lose sight of that affecta unhealthy habits have on our health, which impacts everyone and everything else that matters most to us.

Note: "...workaholics often suffer sleep deprivation which results in impaired brain and cognitive function ..."- The Human Brain—Sleep and Stress, authored by the Franklin Institute in Philadelphia, PA.

God designed sleep to do some wonderful things for us, so take advantage of that.

Proverbs 3:24 (AMP)

"When you lie down, you shall not be afraid; yes, you shall lie down, and your sleep shall be sweet."

Psalms 127:1-2 (AMP)

"A Song of Ascents. Of Solomon. Except the Lord builds the house, they labor in vain who build it; except the Lord keeps the city, the watchman wakes but in vain. It is vain for you to rise up early, to take rest late, to eat the bread of [anxious] toil—for He gives [blessings] to His beloved in sleep."

Matthew 11:28-30 (AMP)

"Come to Me, all you who labor and are heavy-laden and overburdened, and I will cause you to rest. [I will ease and relieve and refresh your souls.] Take My yoke upon you and learn of Me, for I am gentle (meek) and humble (lowly) in heart, and you will find rest (relief and ease and refreshment and recreation and blessed quiet) for your souls. For My yoke is wholesome (useful, good—not harsh, hard, sharp, or pressing, but comfortable, gracious, and pleasant), and My burden is light and easy to be borne."

When we choose to go without sleep in order to complete an assignment, our actions, attitude and appearance may not be a welcoming reflection of the Lord. Not only do we yield to the temptation to neglect God-given sleep, but we are also tempted to publicize our so-called valiant efforts to suffer sleep loss in order to seek the rewards of men. The Scripture below demonstrates this:

Matthew 6:16-18 (AMP)

"And whenever you are fasting, do not look gloomy and sour and dreary like the hypocrites, for they put on a dismal countenance, that their fasting may be apparent to and seen by men. Truly I say to you, they have their reward in full already. But when you fast, perfume your head and wash your face, so that your fasting may not be noticed by men but by your Father, Who sees in secret; and your Father, Who sees in secret, will reward you in the open."

Why do you think it is so hard to suffer silently? _____

_____

What is the reward Jesus refers to in Matthew 6:16? _____

_____

When we make sacrifices, whose reward should we seek? _____

Be responsible by getting the rest you need; otherwise, you run the risk of giving God's work "negative press" and influencing others to believe that His yoke is NOT easy and His burden is NOT light after all.

THE "F" WORD – FAMILY

Do I really have to deal with them? Yes, you do!!!

Matthew 12:46-50 (NKJV)

"While He was still talking to the multitudes, behold, His mother and brothers stood outside, seeking to speak with Him. Then one said to Him, 'Look, Your mother and Your brothers are standing outside, seeking to speak with You.' But He answered and said to the one who told Him, 'Who is My mother and who are My brothers?' And He stretched out His hand toward His disciples and said, "Here are My mother and My brothers! For whoever does the will of My Father in heaven is My brother and sister and mother.'"

God uses family in Kingdom work. Andrew and Peter were brothers. James and John were brothers. Mary and Elizabeth were cousins. Moses, Aaron and Miriam were all siblings. Paul's nephew saved his life.

Acts 23:16 (AMP)

"But the son of Paul's sister heard of their intended attack, and he went and got into the barracks and told Paul."

TAKE AARON AND HIS SONS:

Just as it is in business, ministry with family can be a tremendous reward or a terrible disaster. Here are some tips to help navigate the family/ministry dynamic:

○ As the song says, "If it don't fit, don't force it!"- Don't force your children or spouse into a traditional mold. Instead, encourage them to discover their own place in ministry.

○ Keep expectations clear - If your family members are under your direction, don't hesitate to communicate when standards are not being met.

○ Carry your own load - Help your family to succeed; however, resist the urge to feel condemnation for their bad behavior or pride in their good conduct

Galatians 6:5 (AMP)

"For every person will have to bear (be equal to understanding and calmly receive) his own [little] load [of oppressive faults]."

NOW YOU KNOW

✓ When we turn all of our attention to one area of our lives, we can leave other areas vulnerable.

✓ You are responsible for your part. God will do His.

✓ Trusting God with the things you value most is one of the highest levels of faith.

✓ When called to sacrifice, resist the temptation to publicize your pain. God will reward you.

✓ There are no child labor laws in the Kingdom.

✓ Allow your family to enjoy the benefits of your service.

SEEK TO BE MEEK

Giving sincere thanks to God is an act of meekness, and doing so, whether publicly or privately, we declare our dependence on Him rather than on ourselves. The world, however, has a tendency to confuse meekness with weakness and pridefulness with courage—a trap that seeks to ensnare the unsuspecting. Believers that study the Bible learn that true humility is realizing that God is ultimately responsible for any and everything we accomplish that is good and worthwhile. The very breath we breathe is from God, starting with Adam in the Garden (Genesis 2:7); all wisdom, knowledge and understanding comes from the Lord (Proverbs 2:6-8); and Jesus clearly stated that without Him, we can't do anything (John 15:5). With these and many other scripture verses in mind, we must always endeavor to "seek to be meek" while setting Godly examples to serve, lead and love others.

THE HAGAR TEST

The "Hagar test" is a test of your humility and obedience when you think you are right and they are dead wrong.

Genesis 16:9 (MSG)

"The angel of God said, "Go back to your mistress. Put up with her abuse."

Recall a time when you felt your leader was wrong and you were right. Did you feel contempt for him/her? Did you speak out and defend your position? Did you take matters into your own hands? Did you keep quiet and bear the burden regardless of who was right and who was wrong?

In such a scenario, how do you think contempt for a leader can damage one's ability to fulfill his assignment?

_____

_____

_____

_____

How does the dictionary define contempt?

_____

_____

How does the dictionary define meekness?

_____

_____

Ownership vs. Stewardship

A successful team member masters both ownership and stewardship.

TAKING OWNERSHIP

Luke 12:42 (ESV)

"And the Lord said, 'Who then is the faithful and wise manager whom his master will set over his household to give them their portion of food at the proper time?'"

Elements of ownership include:

o   Make decisions

o   Demonstrate a vested interest

(fill in the blanks)

- ○ _____

- ○ _____

MAINTAIN STEWARDSHIP

Colossians 3:23 (ESV)

"Whatever you do, work heartily, as for the Lord and not for men..."

Elements of stewardship include:

- ○ Use the owner's blueprint

- ○ Build to the owner's specifications

(fill in the blanks)

- ○ _____

- ○ _____

AFFLICTION + HUMILIATION = MEEKNESS

God sometimes allows humiliation for just that reason, to humble us. It breaks that spirit of pride off of us, while also lessening the value of the opinions of others.

Psalms 119:165 (AMP)

"Great peace have they who love your law; nothing shall offend them or make them stumble."

The temptation to lash out when offended can be overwhelming! Being afflicted is highly offensive, especially when others are privy to the situation. Resisting the temptation to lash out is admirable, but internalizing the offense is not good either. What other alternative might a leader have?

_____

_____

_____

How can being offended cause a leader to stumble?

_____

_____

_____

What does loving the "law" in Psalm 119:165 have to do with avoiding offense? (Keep in mind the law on tablets for the Old Testament believer is now the leading of the Holy Spirit for the New Testament believer.)

_____

_____

_____

1 Peter 5:10 (AMP)

"And after you have suffered a little while, the God of all grace [Who imparts all blessing and favor], Who has called you to His [own] eternal glory in Christ Jesus, will Himself complete and make you what you ought to be, establish and ground you securely, and strengthen, and settle you."

According to this scripture, what are the results of enduring suffering well?

_____

_____

POWER UNDER CONTROL

Meekness empowers you to stay in control of your thoughts, words, and actions.

Matthew 26:52 (AMP)

"Then Jesus said to him, 'Put your sword back into its place, for all who draw the sword will die by the sword.'"

Don't be surprised when Jesus says to you, "Put away your sword. Close your mouth. Don't send that email. Hang up the phone."

Was there ever a time when you didn't control your power and later regretted it? How did you feel 5 minutes afterwards?

_____

_____

_____

Describe how you felt 5 hours after that same incident.

_____

_____

_____

Romans 12:19 (AMP)

"Beloved, never avenge yourselves, but leave the way open for [God's] wrath; for it is written, Vengeance is Mine, I will repay (requite), says the Lord."

According to Romans 12:19, whose role are you playing when you attempt to avenge yourself?

_____

Look up the word "meekness" and write the definition:

_____

YOUR KINGDOM IS NOT OF THIS WORLD

Passing the Hagar test allows God to build your character so He can use you for Kingdom purposes.

Matthew 4:3 (AMP)

"And the tempter came and said to Him, 'If You are God's Son, command these stones to be made [loaves of] bread.'"

Luke 23:39 (AMP)

"One of the criminals who was suspended kept up a railing at Him, saying, 'Are You not the Christ (the Messiah)? Rescue Yourself and us [from death]! "

What do these two situations have in common? Can you recognize them in your own life?

_____

_____

_____

Matthew 27:41-42 (KJV)

"Likewise also the chief priests mocking him, with the scribes and elders, said, He saved others; himself he cannot save. If he be the King of Israel, let him now come down from the cross, and we will believe him."

If Jesus had come down from the cross, do you think His enemies would have believed in Him? Why or why not?

_____

_____

_____

✓ **God is able to deal with them.**

✓ **If it was God who called you, it will be God who releases you.**

✓ **Meekness is shown in your ability to control your own power.**

✓ **Never sacrifice your future in a temporary situation.**

✓ *"But the meek [in the end] shall inherit the earth and shall delight themselves in the abundance of peace."* **Psalms 37:11 (AMP)**

LET GOD BE GOD

Remotes are wonderful devices when used for the purposes intended; however, we all know it would be absurd to use a TV remote to open a garage door. Why, then, are so many of us tempted to use our jobs or positions for purposes that were never intended?

ARE YOU USING THE RIGHT REMOTE?

Malachi 3:11 (KJV)

"...neither shall your vine cast her fruit before the time in the field, saith the LORD of hosts."

Bearing fruit in the right season is critical, both naturally and spiritually speaking. While there may be occasions that call for premature fruit to fill an immediate need, the outcome is generally not so good. It is not God's desire that our vine cast its fruit before the time it is intended. In the process of being matured, we can easily find ourselves in the wrong place at the wrong time if not careful. In so doing, we might be tempted to use skills that aren't meant for that season of our lives--much like using a remote for the wrong purpose.

Recall a scenario where you have used the "wrong remote" though your intentions were well-meaning. Briefly describe how that affected you or the people you served.

_____

_____

_____

_____

HELP ME, I'M FALLING!

The Plan of God and the building of His Kingdom are worth any sacrifice He requires you to make.

Matthew 19:29 (Amp)

"And anyone and everyone who has left houses or brothers or sisters or father or mother or children or lands for My name's sake will receive many [even a hundred] times more and will inherit eternal life."

Many church folks—leaders and laypeople alike—are inspired by sermons that provide hope. They should be! We eagerly focus on the idea of becoming prosperous in every aspect of our lives as the memories of scriptural happy endings linger in our minds. Far too often our selective hearing neglects to embrace the painful trials and tribulations that strengthened faith and rendered growth so that God's people would be positioned to receive the blessings. There was plenty of temptation to go around; and like saints today, many yielded miserably because, let's face it, doing so made life seem easier. However, some stayed the course while sacrificing much, even when their lives were at stake!

Read the above Scripture verse in its context and explain why it was necessary for Jesus to make that statement.

_____

_____

_____

Why do you believe the pressures that God's people endured throughout the Old and New Testaments are important for us to hear, read, study, embrace and apply to our own lives, particularly in leadership roles?

_____

_____

_____

Life is wonderful and praise is plentiful when the blessings are flowing our way, but suppose you find yourself suddenly feeling as if you are falling down a mountainside, hitting every rock, bumping every tree and rolling over every angry animal on the way? How have you prepared spiritually and mentally if a crisis (financial, debilitating illness, etc.) were to blindside your family?

_____

_____

_____

If you have not yet prepared yourself, what should you begin to do today that will help strengthen your faith and keep you from becoming bitter if/when confronted with life-changing adversity?

_____

_____

_____

A LESSON IN PURPOSE

If you do not know the purpose of a thing, abuse is inevitable. . . When you look to anything else to give what only God can give, you will eventually abuse and grow to detest the cheap substitute.

-Dr. Miles Munroe

We must never lose sight of the fact that it is our ministry—not the work itself—that is directly related to God. Regardless of the vocation, we are there to serve others, honoring God and representing Christ Jesus from the time we check in until the time we check out. It is a divine system and should cause others to want what we have simply by observing our lives. When the line that divides these two becomes blurred, it is difficult to serve people (work) and use our gifts (ministry) to the fullest. As a result, we negate the effectiveness of this glorious perpetual system designed by God.

Based on what your experience, what do you think is the purpose of work?

o   To exercise our gifts

o   To build our character

o   To provide financial seed for us to sow

o   All of the above

Another challenge for believers in ministry is maintaining a distinction between the work you do to serve others and your relationship with God Himself. Answer the following questions that pertain to working scenarios:

Should the time you spend studying to teach a class or to deliver a message take the place of your personal time with the Bible for your own maturity?

Yes

No

Do you think attending corporate prayer meetings is a good substitute for your daily time in prayer with God?

Yes

No

LOOKING FOR LOVE

When you are in need of love, it is both unscriptural and unwise to look to your work to receive it.

1 John 4:7-8 (NKJV)

"Beloved, let us love one another, for love is of God. . . for God is love."

While it is mandated by God to love others, we must learn how to maintain a healthy relationship when working for and serving others in our ministry roles. Finding that balance can be challenging, especially for those whose idea of love is, for whatever reason, equated with their ability to perform well. What do you think is likely to happen when people who view love in this way under-perform?

_____

_____

_____

_____

_____

_____

If your ultimate goal is to serve, what should your response be when someone you are serving doesn't seem to appreciate your performance?

_____

_____

John 13:35 (AMP)

"By this shall all [men] know that you are My disciples, if you love one another [if you keep on showing love among yourselves]."

Jesus said the defining characteristic of His disciples would be how we love one another. This is how the world will know that we belong to Him. Yet, there are times when we ourselves can't tell who is a follower of Christ and who is not because of the lack of love and care demonstrated. What should we do to make a difficult situation better while serving others?

o   Demand that others love and care for you because that's what the Bible says

o   Tell yourself "I'm just here to work" and ignore everybody

o   Pray, leave the matter to God, and strive to be a team player regardless of the situation

So how do we handle our need to be loved?

We receive the love of God from our relationship with Him through prayer, meditation, and the reading of His Word—His love letter to us. Recognizing how much God loves us literally changes the way we view everyone. Knowing this, we can celebrate ourselves!

When God reveals His perfect, present, persistent love to you, how will it make a difference in you and your ministry?

_____

_____

_____

Read and meditate on Galatians 6:7 and Luke 6:38. How are these Scripture verses applicable to you in your work environment and relationships?

_____

_____

_____

SELF-WORTH

Work is performance-related and your employer has every right to determine the value of your contribution and compensate you accordingly; however, your leader's value of your WORK is certainly not a reflection of the value of YOU.

Jeremiah 1:5 (AMP)

"Before I formed you in the womb I knew [and] approved of you [as My chosen instrument], and before you were born I separated and set you apart, consecrating you; [and] I appointed you as a prophet to the nations."

God has already determined the worth of every human being on the planet. He thought we were so valuable that He sent His only begotten Son, Jesus, to die for us and to make us righteous by His holy standards. It doesn't matter how others view us, God thinks we are beyond great!

Look at the above Scripture again. Was Jeremiah valuable to God because of his performance?

    Yes

    No

What is the danger in relating your self-worth to your work performance?

_____

_____

_____

It is definitely important to strive for top-notch performance, but what should be the appropriate underlying motive be when serving others?

_____

_____

_____

When you look to your workplace to determine your self-worth, you put yourself on an emotional roller coaster that rises or falls with the opinions of others.

God, the ultimate Parent, is not looking at our performance to determine the self-worth of His people. Just like we love our children, regardless of their flaws and how often they mess up, He continues to hold us in high esteem—not because of what we do, but because of what Jesus did; it was HIS performance that makes us look good! However, because we profess to belong to God, we must always strive to represent Him in every way.

Hebrews 11:6 (NKJV)

"But without faith it is impossible to please Him, for he who comes to God must believe that He is, and that He is a rewarder of those who diligently seek Him."

How might faith be a factor when it comes to our self-worth and work performance?

_____

_____

_____

Are we more valuable to God because we work in ministry? Explain your answer.

_____

_____

_____

_____

How does your work in ministry affect others?

_____

_____

_____

Ministry is all about servanthood and helping others to grow. Sometimes titles and status obtained by church leaders can get in the way of their thinking. Why is humility in this line of work so important?

_____

_____

_____

FINANCIAL SUPPLY

It is imperative for ministry workers to recognize that the same spiritual principles concerning finances that apply to the body of Christ, also apply to us.

Ephesians 4:28 (AMP)

"Let the thief steal no more, but rather let him be industrious, making an honest living with his own hands, so that he may be able to give to those in need."

It is unfortunate that so many believers have been taught that our physical sacrifice may at times substitute for our financial sacrifice. While giving has nothing to do with salvation, it has everything to do with our financial covenant with God and our ability (or inability) to trust Him. Among so many other Scriptures, Ephesians 4 provides excellent principles for God's ministry leaders. Intensely study that chapter, realizing that as believers we are called to come up higher in our behavior.

Look at Ephesians 4:28 and describe how new believers should act concerning our work ethic.

_____

_____

_____

Focusing on this same verse, why do you think it is important to give consistently?

_____

_____

_____

We must understand that our job is not our source of financial supply. Who is our source according to Philippians 4:13?

_____

_____

_____

Mark 4:26-27 (AMP)

"The kingdom of God is like a man who scatters seed upon the ground, and then continues sleeping and rising night and day while the seed sprouts and grows and increases—he knows not how."

It is not for us to figure out how God will supply our need. We are believers in His principles, and that includes the Biblical concept of "seedtime and harvest" (Genesis 8:22). We mustn't worry about how, when and where; just trust God, be obedient, and sow the seed, for He is faithful.

Hearing and providing "offering" messages can be difficult for staff members and servant leaders, as is changing our attitudes to conform with the Word and setting examples for others. How will you help those who have been challenged in the area of giving?

NOW YOU KNOW

✓ There are gifts and callings in you that will be seen only in their appointed season or field. Look forward to it!

✓ Do not focus on what you are giving up to obey God. Focus on the harvest He has in mind for you.

✓ If you are not getting your needs met, maybe you are looking to the wrong source.

✓ If you don't know the purpose of a thing, abuse is inevitable – Dr. Miles Munroe

✓ Your work is not your God!

✓ In servant-leadership, love is often one-way. It flows from God through you and out to others.

✓ A leader's motive for performing at their highest level is to serve others and glorify God.

✓ God wants you to prosper.

✓ Do not wait for others to celebrate you. Celebrate your own wonderful self!

DON'T STRIKE THE ROCK

People throughout the world, in every religion, have heard of the renowned character called Moses, even if they have never read the Holy Bible. He is famous for having led millions of people out of Egypt and into the Promised Land. If you have been a leader at any level, you are well aware that dealing with people can be quite a challenge, and Moses was no stranger to challenges as his mission took forty long years. Leading others can wear on anyone's nerves and being called by God doesn't exempt us from the emotional strain that accompanies that position. Consequently, it is in our best interest to lean upon the Lord for EVERYTHING, great and small. If not, we will inevitably become fed up with those we are trying to lead and, like Moses, find ourselves striking the rock over and over again!

YOU'RE FIRED!

Have you ever been pushed over the edge?

Numbers 20:9-11 (NKJV)

"Moses took the rod from before the Lord as He commanded him. And Moses and Aaron gathered the assembly together before the rock; and he said to them, 'Hear now, you rebels! Must we bring water for you out of this rock?' Then Moses lifted his hand and struck the rock twice with his rod; and water came out abundantly, and the congregation and their animals drank."

Sometimes the carnality of others can cause even the meekest leaders to behave out of character. Moses was a leader with a big job to do. Add to that the loss of his sister and the constant complaining of the people, and it's easy to understand how he reached his breaking point. Can you recall a time when you lost your temper and "struck the rock" so to speak? Describe that time below.

_____

_____

_____

Just like colliding weather conditions, when a leader's internal pressure clashes with the pressure of his environment, a storm can form. How do you protect yourself and others when you are vulnerable to losing it?

_____

_____

_____

HE MISREPRESENTED GOD

Numbers 20:12 (AMP)

"And the Lord said to Moses and Aaron, 'Because you did not believe in (rely on, cling to) Me to sanctify Me in the eyes of the Israelites, you therefore shall not bring this congregation into the land which I have given them.'"

Leaders often represent the character of God to their people. Take the word "represent" and make it "re-present" or "to present again." Now, think about some nationally-known leaders in the community of faith. How could a public lapse in their character hurt the church?

_____

_____

_____

HE DIDN'T BELIEVE GOD

James 1:19-20 (AMP)

"Understand [this], my beloved brethren. Let every man be quick to hear [a ready listener], slow to speak, slow to take offense and to get angry. For man's anger does not promote the righteousness God [wishes and requires]."

God instructed Moses to simply speak to the rock. Instead, Moses (led by anger instead of God) spoke to the people and struck the rock. God knows each of us individually and knows exactly what we need in every moment. Have you ever second guessed God's way of dealing with people? According to James our anger does not produce righteousness in others. What do you think it actually produces?

_____

_____

_____

HE DID NOT SANCTIFY GOD IN THE EYES OF THE PEOPLE

Luke 9:54-56 (AMP)

"And when His disciples James and John observed this, they said, 'Lord, do You wish us to command fire to come down from heaven and consume them, even as Elijah did?' But He turned and rebuked and severely censured them. He said, 'You do not know of what sort of spirit you are, for the Son of Man did not come to destroy men's lives, but to save them [from the penalty of eternal death].' And they journeyed on to another village."

John 3:17 (AMP)

"For God did not send the Son into the world in order to judge (to reject, to condemn, to pass sentence on) the world, but that the world might find salvation and be made safe and sound through Him."

In the Old Testament, Elijah called down fire and then slew the prophets of Baal (I Kings 18). Why did Jesus forbid James and John to perform a similar act in Luke 9?

_____

_____

_____

I WANT YOU TO WHUP HER!

Jonah 4:1-3 (AMP)

"But it displeased Jonah exceedingly and he was very angry. And he prayed to the Lord and said, 'I pray You, O Lord, is not this just what I said when I was still in my country? That is why I fled to Tarshish, for I knew that You

are a gracious God and merciful, slow to anger and of great kindness, and [when sinners turn to You and meet Your conditions] You revoke the [sentence of] evil against them. Therefore now, O Lord, I beseech You, take my life from me, for it is better for me to die than to live.'"

The great prophet Jonah was practically suicidal after the Lord revoked the sentence of evil against the Nineveh. Often leaders use God's "anger" as a control mechanism for people. Nineveh repented and God's anger was withheld. How could God's mercy be a detriment to Jonah's influence in Israel?

_____

_____

Imagine if God had destroyed Nineveh. How do you think Jonah would have responded?

_____

_____

Would God have been happy to destroy Nineveh?

_____

_____

GOD'S VALUE SYSTEM

Luke 12:6-7 (AMP)

"Are not five sparrows sold for two pennies? And [yet] not one of them is forgotten or uncared for in the presence of God. But [even] the very hairs of your head are all numbered. Do not be struck with fear or seized with alarm; you are of greater worth than many [flocks] of sparrows."

PEOPLE ARE PRECIOUS TO GOD

God is interested in how we treat people who (seemingly) can do nothing for us. At the same time, God expects us to be good stewards of our time. As your influence grows as a leader, you will attract many people. Some will come to grow, and some will come for show.

How can you properly discern when others are sincere or merely wasting your time?

1 Corinthians 9:27 (AMP)

"But [like a boxer] I buffet my body [handle it roughly, discipline it by hardships] and subdue it, for fear that after proclaiming to others the Gospel and things pertaining to it, I myself should become unfit [not stand the test, be unapproved and rejected as a counterfeit]."

NOW YOU KNOW

✓ Just because your patience has run out does not mean that God's has.

✓ We misrepresent God when we mistreat people from our leadership position.

✓ It takes faith to trust and follow God's direction where people are concerned.

✓ It is imperative that we as leaders sanctify God in the eyes of those we lead. Always present His heart.

✓ Examine your heart for the best interest of the people.

✓ No matter how talented and gifted you are, without God you can do nothing. Doing nothing is not an option.

✓ God knows who to whup! And He won't do it for our satisfaction.

BOW OUT GRACEFULLY

Regardless of whether we acquire relationships through ministry, the workplace, recreationally, or in the home, there comes a time when change must occur. It is inevitable. How we handle the challenge of change is critical to the next phase of our status, whatever that may be. The attitude we pursue in dealing with changes that drive our lives to new heights or disappointing lows will have a lasting effect on those who are most likely to be directly impacted as we, for whatever reason, walk away from one relationship, only to walk into another. In preparing for life's changes, the wise choice is to pursue diligently an attitude of humility through the reading of God's Word; this enables us to bow out gracefully from any given situation when the time presents itself. The alternative is to ignore God's trustworthy principles, which leaves many believers ill-prepared and they sometimes storm out grudgingly, not realizing the possibilities for growth and the opportunity to exemplify God's love and grace.

Every individual mentioned in the Bible—from the first Adam to the Last Adam (Jesus) and everyone in between—sets some kind of example for us today. Their lives provide talking points that are designed to teach us how to live by learning from and trusting in God. Explain what you think Solomon teaches us in Ecclesiastes.

Ecclesiastes 3:1

" To everything there is a season, and a time for every matter or purpose under heaven:"

_____

_____

_____

Why would it be important for an orientation in ministry to include a graceful exit strategy?

_____

_____

_____

How would you administrate a God-ordained change of season in your own life?

_____

_____

_____

_____

TIMING IS EVERYTHING; DON'T BE A PREEMIE

God uses the circumstances of one season to develop us for the next season.

It is an understatement to say that ministry is not easy. In fact, the Bible is filled with the hazards of "going into all the world" preaching, teaching, and trying to convince people that God's gospel is true and life in Christ Jesus really is a wonderful thing! The early church had it rough enough facing persecution outside the church, but a lot of their woes came from within. Varying behaviors and perspectives are learned from birth, as we are products of our environments. Consequently, our viewpoints and attitudes can differ dramatically, which often leads to conflict, particularly when in close quarters. Such conflicts can tempt us to drop everything and run for the hills—and many. . . do just that.

Think of just one situation in ministry that caused you to run for the hills. Why do you think your decision to leave might have been premature?

_____

_____

What do you believe would help you make a better decision the next time a difficult situation arises?

_____

_____

_____

READ THE SIGNS

There are two signs to watch for when you believe it is time for a change of assignment: 1) the grace of God will lift, and 2) your replacement will appear on the scene.

1 Corinthians 15:10 (KJV)

"But by the grace of God I am what I am: and his grace which was bestowed upon me was not in vain; but I laboured more abundantly than they all: yet not I, but the grace of God which was with me."

It is unfortunate that society as a whole has been conditioned to readily view any act of replacement as a negative. The fact is sometimes the negative view is warranted—an object wears out and is no longer effectively serving the purpose for which it was intended, so the reasonable thing to do is replace it. People, however, should learn never to equate themselves with worn out, inanimate objects. By God's grace, we are made in His image, filled with purpose and ever useful whether our situations change for better or for worse! Viewing replacement from this perspective can prepare your heart for a more positive experience when you see the signs of change approaching.

Meditate on 1 Corinthians 15:10. Applying it to yourself, why should you be confident about your current assignment?

_____

_____

_____

If you think of the meaning of grace, what do you suppose is the sole purpose of your current position.

_____

_____

_____

Read 1 Kings 19:16 and John 3:30, and then imagine having to find a replacement for yourself. What should your attitude be?

_____

_____

WILLING TO DECREASE

When your time comes to bow out gracefully, you may not go out with a bang and a big crowd. You may go out quietly as your role in that assignment becomes less prominent.

John 3:30 (AMP)

"He must increase, but I must decrease. [He must grow more prominent; I must grow less so.]"

John the Baptist was as humble as he was powerful when it came to walking in his purpose. When it was time for him to step back (decrease), by God's grace he willfully submitted. However, we discover that even a man as great as John began to have doubts when he found himself imprisoned. While John, no doubt, didn't feel very good about himself or his change of venue, what was Jesus saying about him to others (Matthew 11:11)?

_____

_____

_____

In our humanness, we all have doubts especially when we do all we know to do, yet another comes to take our place. What advice would you give to someone in this situation?

_____

_____

_____

DON'T LEAVE FOR THE WRONG REASONS

Another way to gauge the timing of your bowing out is to examine carefully your reasons for leaving. Here are some definite red flags: 1) Don't leave for money, and 2) don't leave in strife.

Ephesians 4:28 (NKJV)

"Let him who stole steal no longer, but rather let him labor, working with his hands what is good, that he may have something to give him who has need."

Living in a world that is heavily influenced by the Prince of Darkness, even believers in Christ Jesus fall prey to the tactics of the devil. These cunning schemes include the temptation to lose sight not only of the One who supplies our every need, but also of our purpose for acquiring financial resources. If your current salary is considerably lower than the skill sets you've achieved, describe how you might be encouraged to stay in that position after reading Mark 4:24-28, Isaiah 55:10, and 2 Corinthians 9:10?

James 3:16 (KJV)

"For where envying and strife is, there is confusion and every evil work."

Look up the word strife and write the definition:

_____

_____

_____

Meditate on Proverbs 30:32-33, then recall a situation in your leadership role where strife was a factor that caused you to want to leave. What did you learn from that situation?

_____

_____

_____

ESSENTIALS OF PREPARATION FOR LIFTOFF: LEADER, FAMILY & YOU

Our loving Father has provided us with a myriad of spiritual tools (Biblical principles) that serve to equip every believer in every situation of life. Leaving environments in which we've become established and comfortable is no exception. While our reasons for leaving may vary, we never want to burn any bridges when making that final exit. After all, your departure could very well serve as your "liftoff" depending on how you say good-bye. What should be the first action you take when realizing a certain chapter in your life is coming to a close?

o   Blast your plans on Facebook and Twitter

o   Seek God for a strategic exit plan and wisdom on how to prepare key people in your life

What do you think is the best way to prepare your Pastor or ministry leader?

o   Tell him/her privately in person if at all possible.

o   Ask to be released from your position.

o   Offer to give your leader a reasonable amount of time to replace you.

o   Offer to train a replacement.

o   All of the above.

Is it really necessary to prepare your children?

o   No, not really.

o   Absolutely!

How can children at any age be negatively impacted by not being informed?

o   They may be confused concerning your relationship with God.

o   Resentment and bitterness towards your former co-workers

o   Both

Though our heads may be reeling at the possibility of leaving a once-established position, it can help to know ahead of time the emotions we might experience during that awkward transition period, and that through prayer and in due time these feelings will certainly pass. Which of the following best describe how you felt/feel in a similar situation?

o   Feel queasy at the thought of losing certain privileges

o   Alienated

o   Unimportant

o   Unsure of yourself

o   All of the above

THE BEST OF TIMES AND THE WORST OF TIMES

Sometimes our best intentions encounter interference and things do not always go as we plan.

God's prophet Nehemiah was a wonderful example of how to bow out gracefully from a position. He held the prestigious position of cupbearer to the king. Though he was a Jewish slave, he spent a lot of time in the presence of royalty. However, when hearing about the dire situation in Jerusalem, he knew it was time to go.

What did Nehemiah do before approaching the king (see Nehemiah 1)?

_____

_____

_____

David, that wonderful psalmist, also had a relationship with a king and, like Nehemiah, he had an exemplary prayer life. Both kings encountered God's grace, but only one—Artaxerxes—was willing to walk in it. King Saul established David in a position of authority, but his insane jealousy left David with no other alternative than to leave, forcing him to go from the best of times to the worst of times. Though David ran for his life from King Saul for many years, he remained loyal to him and his family.

What lesson(s) can be learned from David's relationship with Saul that will prepare us to bow out gracefully when the time comes?

_____

_____